A QUICK GUIDE TO

Teaching Persuasive Writing

K–2

Other Books in the Workshop Help Desk Series

A Quick Guide to
Reaching Struggling Writers, K–5
M. COLLEEN CRUZ

A Quick Guide to
Making Your Teaching Stick, K–5
SHANNA SCHWARTZ

A Quick Guide to
Boosting English Acquisition in Choice Time, K–2
ALISON PORCELLI AND CHERYL TYLER

For more information about these and other titles,
visit www.firsthand.heinemann.com.

A QUICK GUIDE TO
Teaching Persuasive Writing
K–2

SARAH PICARD TAYLOR

Workshop Help Desk Series
Edited by Lucy Calkins
with the Teachers College Reading and Writing Project

HEINEMANN
Portsmouth, NH

An imprint of Heinemann
361 Hanover Street
Portsmouth, NH 03801–3912
www.heinemann.com

Offices and agents throughout the world

© 2008 by Sarah Picard Taylor

Library of Congress Cataloging-in-Publication Data
Taylor, Sarah Picard.
  A quick guide to teaching persuasive writing, K–2 / Sarah Picard Taylor.
      p. cm. — (Workshop help desk series)
  Includes bibliographical references.
  ISBN 13: 978–0–325–02597–1
  ISBN 10: 0–325–02597–5
  1. English language—Composition and exercises—Study and teaching
(Early childhood). I. Title.
  LB1139.5.L35.T39 2008
  372.62′3049—dc22   2008027305

SERIES EDITOR: *Lucy Calkins and the Teachers College Reading and Writing Project*
EDITOR: *Kate Montgomery*
PRODUCTION: *Elizabeth Valway*
COVER DESIGN: *Jenny Jensen Greenleaf*
COVER PHOTO: *Angela Jimenez*
INTERIOR DESIGN: *Jenny Jensen Greenleaf*
COMPOSITION: *House of Equations, Inc.*
MANUFACTURING: *Steve Bernier*

Printed in the United States of America on acid-free paper
12 11 10 09   VP   2 3 4 5

To Bob and Terry Picard

*The courage needed to revise and edit this book seemed small
compared with the courage you gathered this year. Thank you
for teaching me to laugh, work hard, and empathize.
I am proud to have come from both of you.*

CONTENTS

ACKNOWLEDGMENTS

Lucy Calkins and the entire Teachers College Reading and Writing Project community have supported my efforts to write this book. Lucy persuaded others that this book needed to be written and trusted me with the topic. She also gave me generous feedback as I drafted and revised. I am honored to have written with such an admired writer and mentor. Maggie Beattie was my writing companion for this book. All first-time authors should have the blessing of her dedication. Laurie Pessah, Kathleen Tolan, Amanda Hartman, and Mary Ehrenworth, our leaders at the Reading and Writing Project, modeled for me how a staff developer can support teachers in schools as well as carve out time for writing. Their feedback, kindness, and generosity are in the pages of this book. My colleagues in the TCRWP community, including Rebecca Cronin, Dahlia Dallal, Brooke Geller, Cory Gillette, Christine Holley, Monique Knight, Lauren Kolbeck, Natalie Louis, Enid Martinez, Beth Moore, Marika Paez, Allison Porcelli, Shanna Schwartz, Karma Suttles, and Tonya White, supported me with conversations about persuasive writing. Carl Anderson has always supported my efforts to write and I am thankful for his encouragement. The teachers at P.S. 102, P.S. 134, P.S. 29, P.S. 239, and P.S. 130 in New York City and at Horizon School in Sun Prairie, Wisconsin, piloted some of the minilessons described in this book. Charlotte Arboleta, Naomi Berkowitz,

Joel Blecha, Pat Bleichman, Gina Braun, Jeffrey Gross, Colette Hall, Erica Hubbard, Courtney Lauer, Katherine Nigen, Katherina Payne, Kirsten Price, Megan Quirk, Emilie Rosales Trimble, Andrea Raskie, Nicole Santomero, Sarah Scheldt, Liz Sturges, and Andi Wissot read drafts of the minilessons in this book, tried them in their classrooms, collected students' samples for the book, and gave critical feedback. I am thankful for my roots at P.S. 126 and CH Bird School, especially to my classroom partners Sandra Weisel, Jane Kinney, Kristine Kirst, and Amanda Thompson. All of you and so many more gave me the physical space and intellectual companionship to bounce around new ideas. Thanks also to the principals who lead the way: Daria Rigney, Chad Weidemeyer, and Melanie Woods. Thanks to Colleen Cruz, Julia Mooney, and Kate Montgomery for the honest feedback that made my dreams for this book become reality. Thanks to CMG, EMS, and ER for enduring friendships and to my family of Picards, Taylors, Dewiches, and Pfaffs for unconditional support. Tony, for answering all of my high school love letters with humor, and for reminding me that that I could put my heart on the page fifteen years later, thank you.

I grew up in a small midwestern community but I wanted to know the world. I woke up early and rushed home after school to watch the national network news because we did not have cable or the Internet. I had to catch the news when it was actually on television. I loved listening to Secretary of State George Schultz tell about the foreign countries he visited, and I was a huge fan of Tip O'Neil's. I would listen to George talk about the people of Russia as I pulled on my snow pants and moon boots, preparing to brave the long walk to the bus. I admired the way Tip swung the gavel. I watched the news to learn about other places in the world and became aware of all the people I wanted to meet, help, and understand. I was inspired by the labor movement in Poland and was concerned for Libya. I talked about all of this with friends at recess and tried to persuade them to think like me. Yes, right there on the playground, I was talking about trade unions and solidarity and arguing for peace on behalf of the Libyan people. These may have been one-sided conversations, but I thought it was important for my friends to know about these issues. I wanted to persuade them to care as much as I did and do something to make life better for other people.

As I work in classrooms in New York City and across the country, I am reminded each day of the reason I decided to teach—our children have voices that need to be heard. Even five-, six-, and seven-year-olds can learn to be advocates for issues they care about—whether those involve world events, video games, or classroom life. Children can advocate for more pencils or books for their classroom. They can advocate for others too. The seniors at the local senior center may need more magazines. It makes sense, then, to teach a unit of study on persuasive letter writing so students can see their words making a difference. Also, a new version of Monopoly is the best yet, a new restaurant down the block gives free markers while you wait, and the latest Magic Tree House book is unbelievable! It makes sense, then, to teach a unit of study on persuasive review writing so students can see readers believing in and agreeing with their words.

This book is organized to help teach units of study on persuasive writing. The first chapter describes the reasons to try a persuasive writing unit of study. The next two chapters provide two possible persuasive writing units of study for primary classrooms. The final chapter includes tips and ideas to help young writers get their persuasive writing out into the world.

The units described here are written in such a way that they stand on the shoulders of other units in *Units of Study for Primary Writing* (Calkins et al. 2003).

As you read, you might take notes and plan to rally some colleagues to teach these units with you. You will find helpful photos and stories from actual classrooms to help you work through the hard parts.

The units stand on the shoulders of books by Katherine Bomer, Katie Ray, Stephanie Parsons, and Janet Angelillo. In addition, Lucy Calkins and Cory Gillette's work with persuasive essaying for older writers helped me see a line of growth for students.

I wrote this book knowing that most of you reading it already teach in classrooms with ongoing writing workshops and know the ebb and flow of a writing workshop unit of study. The way the lessons are described, with connections, teaching points, active engagements, and links, will feel familiar. However, if you are new to workshop teaching, I invite you to come along on the journey. Read the stories of the teachers and children. I hope you will be persuaded to join us in the writing workshop!

CHAPTER ONE

Persuasive Writing
in the Primary Grades

One morning I walked into Carmella Wittman's sun-lit kindergarten classroom in Sun Prairie, Wisconsin. Something was not right. Only a few children were gathered at their meeting area. The rest sat openmouthed, gazing out the floor-to-ceiling windows.

"It's a bike rodeo, and we can't be in it!" said Hunter. As I looked, he explained that the bike rodeo was a program offered by neighborhood police officers to promote bicycle safety.

"No kindergartners allowed," Hunter continued, "but why can't we be in it?"

No wonder the kids were distracted. They could not help it. The injustice of not being included in the rodeo was staring them in the face.

Teachers are always looking for ways to teach their students to be active citizens, to think independently and try things on their own (Bomer and Bomer 2001). Teachers who hope to channel children toward persuasive writing and who want children to see that writing can be a form of social action can seize upon moments when children perceive that there has been an injustice in their school. When youngsters barge into the classroom after recess, all in a tizzy because of a fight on the playground, or when they argue that a school policy is unfair, I am apt to muse, "I wonder if there is something you could write in writing workshop today that might help you address this problem? Who needs to hear your feelings in order for the problem to be solved? What ideas do you have to solve the problem?" My goal is to teach children that writing can be part of their response to injustice and to teach them, too, that writers mull over possible genres and audiences for persuasive writing. Of course, there are bigger lessons being taught. When we equip our children to write persuasively, we help them go from whining and complaining toward taking positive action. We help them learn that any one individual can make a real-world difference.

Back in Carmella's classroom, I looked at the children gazing out the windows. Carmella and I had been in the middle of a unit of study that asked our students to write true stories from their lives, but I looked at her and said, "You know, Carmella, I think we need to change our plans a little."

In the next few minutes, the youngsters gathered at the meeting area and I said, "Writers, sometimes writers write true stories from their lives, as we've been doing. Sometimes we write for other reasons. Sometimes we write so as to persuade people in charge to do things differently. Because it sounds like many of you are really upset about the bike rodeo, I was wondering if you'd like me to teach you how you can use writing to try to persuade people to change that policy about kindergartners."

"Why can't we be in it?" Hunter asked again. A few of his friends chimed in with "Yeah!" and "It isn't fair!"

"Well, one thing you can do is write a letter to the people in charge and ask them that question. You might be able to change their minds, and if not, at least you might understand their reasons for the policy," I said, silently hoping the principal would not mind the deluge of letters that would soon appear in his mailbox.

In the days that followed, that group of children continued to write and receive letters from the principal, the police officers, and other members of the school staff. When older children in the school heard the buzz about the rodeo letters, they were impressed! Soon letters were flying across the school about wobbly tables, leaky faucets, reading spots that were not working for independent reading, and the need for more books of one kind or another. Teachers began meeting to think about the qualities of effective persuasive writing and to study student work, thinking, "How can we take what our children are doing another step?" That school had officially begun its first persuasive writing unit.

Why Persuasive Writing in the Primary Grades?

My colleagues and I in the Teachers College Reading and Writing Project hope that all primary teachers consider providing children with a unit of study designed to help them write persuasively. Different schools and especially different grade levels of teachers have decided on different ways to teach persuasive writing. Some kindergarten teachers have worked to develop a unit of study that invites children to write signs and posters that affect people's actions. Many primary teachers have embraced the idea of designing a unit of study to help children write persuasive letters. Many other teachers—and especially those in the second grade—have embraced the notion of teaching children to write persuasive reviews. The reviews can be designed to promote or to critique television shows, restaurants, games, and, of course, books. All of these options help children feel their writing can make the world a better place.

My colleagues and I teach persuasive writing in part so children come to know the real-world power of writing. The persuasive writing genre opens opportunities for writers to work on several qualities of good writing. Specifically, persuasive writing requires writers to:

- write with purpose for a selected audience
- decide upon and then elaborate on the most important parts of their message
- write and edit for readers, making sure the text is easy to read

Writing with Purpose for a Selected Audience

When a child yearns for the latest toy, he considers which parent to ask and even weighs the best way to win over that parent. "If you say yes, I'll start taking Toby for a walk every day," one child might promise, eyeing the family's restless pet. "If you don't let me, then I'll never forgive you," another might say, hoping threats will seal the deal. We, as teachers, have the opportunity to tap into children's innate ability to use language to persuade.

In a unit of study on persuasive writing, children will need to learn that their lives are full of reasons to write persuasively. We can expect that their first topics will be centered on their own lives: campaigning for a later bedtime or more time to play video games after school. But as soon as we take students on trips around the neighborhood and help them live their lives seeing injustices and seeing possibilities for goodness, even our youngest writers will discover that they can act on the behalf of others—that writing a persuasive text can improve not just their own lives but the lives of many people. When a cluster of first graders at P.S. 59 grew tired of kickballs hitting their windowpanes and interrupting their learning several times each day, they decided to write a letter. Katherine Nigen taught her students that first they needed to think about whom could help them solve the problem. They considered writing to the principal to "tell on the big kids." However, after some thinking, they considered writing to the teachers of the big kids for the same purpose. Finally, one of students suggested they actually write to the big kids directly, asking them to play more carefully. Needless to say, their letters worked!

Once a writer has decided upon an audience, they need to think carefully about how to convince that specific audience. Children can plan a roleplay. If writers want to argue for longer recess time (or any other cause) they can think, "What reasons might be persuasive if we are arguing this cause to the principal?" or "What reasons might be persuasive if we are arguing for this cause to other children, perhaps in hopes that they'll cosign a petition?" People can assume different roles and role-play an effort to persuade.

When the first graders hoped to persuade older kids to try to keep balls from slamming on the first-grade classrooms' windows, they rehearsed for their letter by asking themselves and each other, "What do we want to say to the big kids?" They pictured the big kids in their minds and thought, "What exactly do they need to know?" As they composed their message on a big piece of chart paper, it was clear these writers had discovered a way to write with focus. (See Figure 1.1.)

Choosing and Then Elaborating on the Most Important Parts of a Message

Just as we teach students to elaborate in their narrative writing, we also want to teach this in persuasive writing. We teach students to think of reasons that their request is important, list each of those reasons, and then, if they can, illustrate each reason with a quick narrative description—just the part of a story that shows the reader why this request is important. Some writers may do this elaboration work through pictures on the page, others through words.

There are many qualities of good writing that are important in every genre, and focus is one of these. If a writer wants to channel a reader to act differently, the writer needs to decide what exactly it is that she wants to say and then work hard to say that one thing. If a writer really wants a dog, then that writer is wise to devote her full attention to explaining the

FIG. 1.1 *First graders at P.S. 59 post a letter to the fifth grade to request the older students not to kick the kickballs into their classroom windows.*

advantages of a dog. As the writer works on this text—presumably a persuasive letter—she might remember experiences with a dog that weren't especially positive. The memory of moments spent scrubbing the rug might come to the writer's mind, but it won't be hard to teach her to choose evidence and details that help advance her cause . . . and to delete distracters.

In a unit of study on persuasive writing, then, the fact that the writer's purpose, the writer's focus, is embodied in a person, a reader, helps teach children the skills of focus and elaboration. Writers are given very real reasons to control their message—to channel their reader!

Writing and Editing with Readers in Mind

A unit of study on persuasive writing gives children reasons to invest themselves zealously in their writing. Children will have real-world reasons to make the stories they tell ones that actually touch readers enough to stir them to action. And children will also have lots of reasons to write as clearly as they can, using all they know about the conventions of written language. The text will be mailed, sent, delivered. Someone will open the envelope, hold the child's letter, and work as hard as possible to decipher what the child has said. The reader will need help, and it is the writer's job to provide that help.

Rules and conventions of written language come to life when a child knows that his text will be passed into the hands of a reader. All of a sudden there is a very real reason to write with end punctuation, to stretch words out and listen to and record as many sounds as possible, to rely on known words to spell unknown words.

This book does not specifically address ways in which a teacher can help children write more conventionally, but I do advise teachers to mail children's actual writing, when possible. Recipients of letters and readers of reviews will know the writers are five- or six- or seven-year-olds and will not expect perfection—and children, in the meantime, will be galvanized to use all they know and can learn to write in ways that reach readers.

What Might Some Units of Study Look Like?

It always helps to be able to imagine the big picture of a unit of study before embarking on the day-by-day sequence of that unit. Of course, a unit on persuasive writing will look very different if writers are kindergartners or if they are second graders. Younger writers may rely on signs and posters to persuade; while more developed writers will be able to write longer texts.

Persuasive Letters Unit

During this unit of study, children will zealously churn out letters that are designed to persuade people to take action. They may request that someone stop or start doing something (see Figures 1.1 and 1.2). Sometimes children will go so far as to suggest new solutions to a problem (see Figure 1.3). Additional

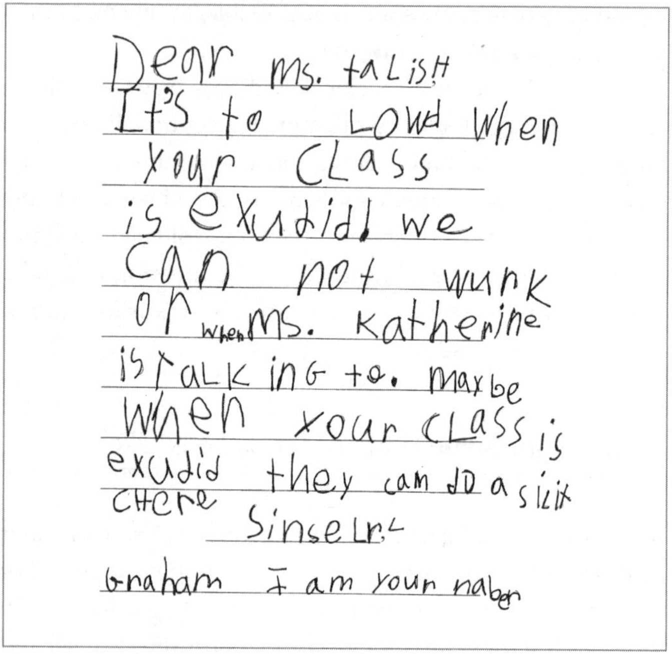

Dear ms. taLisH
It's to LoWd when
your CLass
is exudid we
can not wunk
or when Ms. katherine
is taLking to. maybe
When your CLass is
exudid they can do a siLit
cHere
Sinselr,
Graham I am your naben

FIG. 1.2 *Graham's Letter*

examples of letters and Alexandra's full six-page letter from Figure 1.3 are on our website, www.firsthand.heinemann.com. Of course, sometimes solutions are not so easy to devise, and so a youngster may request to meet to discuss a problem. In all of these letters, children will need to elaborate by providing reasons to back their requests, and often, they may decide to embed little examples into their letters. Of course, children will need to revise and edit with their audience in mind, pushing themselves as writers to make each persuasive letter the very best it can be before it goes out to an audience.

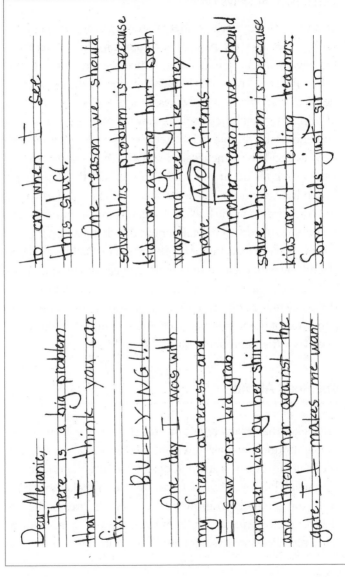

Dear Melanie,

There is a big problem that I think you can fix.

BULLYING!!!

One day I was with my friend at recess and I saw one kid grab another kid by her shirt and threw her against the gate. It makes me want to cry when I see this stuff.

One reason we should solve this problem is because kids are getting hurt both ways and feel like they have NO friends!

Another reason we should solve this problem is because kids aren't telling teachers. Some kids just sit in

FIG. 1.3 *Alexandra's Letter*

11

Persuasive Reviews Unit

This unit will begin with students studying other reviews from online sources, newspapers, and magazines. In Chapter 3, I suggest ways to help children notice the structure of published reviews. Then the chapter explains how to teach students to craft their own reviews. Students first develop lists of things they feel they could review for other people and of audiences who might read the reviews. The young writers will need to decide how they really feel about the subject of the review and consider if the audience will feel the same way. When they begin their reviews, the students will start with a little description of the book, video game, movie, or restaurant and then write specific details about the characters, actors, or food that were pleasing or displeasing. Finally, they will end the review with their opinion of the subject and perhaps consider the circumstances in which a person may want to read the particular book, watch the given movie, play the video game, or eat the mentioned food. (See examples on our website, www.firsthand.heinemann.com.)

The Road Ahead

The pages that follow reflect my investment, belief, and experience around persuasive writing in the primary grades. To think, it all began with a rodeo. I left the experience in Carmella's kindergarten room stronger in my belief that if we want our students to grow up to be active citizens in this democracy, we must teach them to be active citizens from an early age. Primary teachers are integral in this process. We cannot wait for kids to get older and cross our fingers and hope we did our job. Teachers need to carve out opportunities to have young students' voices heard. And heard early.

Students have a sense of passion for the things they love to do. They also have a keen sense of what is fair and unfair. They want to do what is right, and when they see something that makes someone else feel bad, they want to do something to make it better. They are beginning to develop empathy, and we can foster all of this through persuasive writing.

CHAPTER TWO

Writing Persuasive Letters

Writing letters in school too often means the ponderous writing-a-friendly-letter task: writer's address on the right, recipient's address on the left, skipped line before the greeting, perfectly aligned paragraphs, and so on.

We all know, however, that a perfectly skipped line or perfectly chosen greeting is worth nothing if the content of the letter is meaningless to the reader. Letters produced in a letter writing unit of study that do not focus on the content of the message are simply exercises in paragraphing and punctuation. In the name of letter writing, these kinds of lessons teach a proper form of etiquette, not the meaning making that will make a difference to the writer and the reader.

I learned the important lessons in letter writing from my family and friends. My mother, trying to boost my spirits before each painful appointment with Dr. Griggs, my pediatric asthma specialist, would write me a letter reminding me of all the reasons I was brave enough and strong enough to enter his office. My father sent me cards all through college reminding me to keep my dorm room clean and my nose in the books. My parents were the first ones who persuaded me to do many things I was afraid to do. When I was worried about the tests at Dr. Griggs' office or the endless stack of reading lists in college, it was my parents' persuasive words that convinced me I could do more than I thought I could. My mother, father, and I have kept those old letters; the contents matter to us.

I grew up writing letters upon letters. I wrote some to my parents, trying to convince them that I wasn't the one who lost my mom's fancy Fiskars scissors or that I needed to go on the high school ski trip. I wrote letters to my summer camp friends and later to my high school boyfriend, who lived in another Wisconsin community. I learned I could put my hopes and heartaches on the page, seal them up, and send them into the hands of another person, far, far away. I was taught that if I spoke in my very own voice, in ways that matched me perfectly, another person could hold my letter in his hands and feel as if I were right there. I was taught that if I worked really hard on a letter, I could help another person to dream my dreams, to see possibilities she had not imagined, and to begin to act differently.

You may have been equally lucky, growing up with parents and friends who helped you know that letters can change the world. But there are many people in this world whose only lessons in letter writing revolve around greetings and paragraphing. It is important, then, that school provides every child with an opportunity to learn lessons in letter writing that really matter.

Before your year even begins, you'll want to consider which genre you will teach and when you'll teach that genre. As you plan, remember that any genre can be taught in a variety of ways. For example, you could teach letter writing to your kindergartners as part of a larger unit on writing for many purposes, in many forms. Within such a unit, you'd plan to induct children into all the many forms and purposes there are for writing, inviting children to label the classroom with signs, to send cards and letters home to parents, to write books of all sorts, to try their hand at recipes, songs, poems, and so on.

Then again, you could teach a unit on letter writing in which your purpose would be to show children that sometimes writers work together to create something, and you could suggest children plan and institute a schoolwide postal system. The children's writing, then, could involve writing to support a particular endeavor—in this case, the establishment of a schoolwide postal system. Once established, children could write letters that would travel via that postal system. One could imagine such a unit, for example, occurring before a schoolwide effort to send out appreciative valentines to one and all.

This chapter provides an overview of yet another way in which a letter writing unit could unfold, and this particular unit is designed to help children develop the muscles that are essential in persuasive writing. In many schools that work closely with the Teachers College Reading and Writing Project, we introduce persuasive writing in first grade through a monthlong (or three-week) unit on persuasive letter writing, and then the following year, children's abilities to persuade are further extended by a unit on review writing. The following year, children use and extend many of the skills they've been developing, this time writing persuasive literary essays, often arguing for the importance and validity of a claim about a character in a book.

Unit Goals and Overview

One of the most important goals of this unit is to teach children that letter writers see the world as it is, imagine what it could be, and use writing to make dreams come true. On the playground and during classroom altercations, you teach children to use words, not fists, to work out difficulties, and persuasive letters are an extension of this. Because we write, this moves us not only to complain but to take positive action. We imagine solutions, and we write to advance those causes.

Another goal for this unit is to teach children to write their beliefs, their claims, in compelling ways. When children write persuasive letters, they'll aim to rally a reader to believe as they do. Years from now, they'll be asked to write essays in which they advance thesis statements, and one could almost think of this unit as a way for children to become aware of their persuasive writing muscles and get them working a bit.

Equally important, this unit provides a wonderful opportunity to teach children that people can't just say *anything*. Words matter, and therefore it is important for us to choose our words carefully, to take some time deciding on ideas we want to recommend and causes we want to advance, and then to be prepared to support our ideas with evidence. Even six-

and seven-year-olds can learn that after saying, "I think you should . . . ," Or "I think it would be better if . . . ," it is important to provide convincing reasons.

Then as children learn to write ideas or suggestions, backed up with evidence, they'll be learning to write within the structure that underlies all of expository writing. This is no small challenge!

A unit on persuasive writing is tailor-made to teach children what it means to write for an audience. This unit provides children with a chance to consider that the reasons that will convince one audience will not necessarily convince another. They can also learn that the language choices one might make when writing the to president of the United States and those one might make writing to a classmate are different.

It is important to notice that in any unit of study, and especially in any K–2 unit of study, the first goal is to invite children to work zealously and with independence, approximating the new kind of writing they are being asked to do. One could say, in fact, that the first goal is for children to write bad persuasive letters—and to do so with confidence, zeal, purpose, pleasure, and above all, independence. Children need to understand the big work that we're asking them to do and to believe this work is within their grasp, and they need to be able to carry on without step-by-step support—otherwise, we, as teachers, will not have any free hands in order to help individuals along. Here's the overall plan for this particular unit: It will begin with you saying to children, "This month, you'll all have the chance to write lots and lots of letters, and you can write those letters in order to persuade people to do things you believe need to be done." Then, in effect, you will say,

"Here's your fancy writing paper, your envelope—off you go!" Once children are writing and writing, you will, in essence, say, "Now that you guys are writing such important letters, let me share with you a few techniques that will make your letters even more powerful."

Unit Paper and Materials

As with other units of study, you will need to do a little work behind the scenes to prepare for the unit. Alongside all the other paper choices, you will need letter writing paper. You will want to invite students to cocreate some of the paper choices before this unit of study begins. Students can study letters they have received in order to design letter paper. Chances are they'll suggest the paper include a line at the top right corner for the date, a line at the top left for writers to write the greeting, and lots of lines underneath for the message. Many of my colleagues staple two or three pages together so the students know their letters can be multiple pages in length.

The fun will begin for children after you make the lines on the pages. Children can use time during open work or choice time to decorate the borders of the paper with patterns, designs, fingerprints, flowers, and miniature animals. Sarah Scheldt's first-grade class made more formal paper that read, "From the desk of _____," at the top of the page. You can take the decorated pages that the children design and copy them so all the students in the class can use the paper choices their classmates have created. Ceremoniously put these paper choices into the writing center in a few different paper trays so students can choose the stationery that best suits their letter. You may even decide to change the name of your writing center to *stationery shop* and *post office nook* for this unit of study so students know they can go to one area for the different paper choices and then another area to deposit their letters and prepare them for mailing.

The teachers with whom I have worked found that devising a system for collecting addresses, stamps, and for actually mailing the letters is important at the beginning of this unit. We certainly can't have the children writing if there's no place for their letters to go! Teachers can write a letter to the families at the beginning of the unit to explain the new kind of writing the students will make (see Figure 2.1) and enlist family support for getting the letters out into the world. Some of my colleagues also give each student a small address book and ask the student to collect the addresses of people in his or her life. Students take these home and record addresses from their family and neighborhood.

Most teachers also set out a few baskets in the writing center to collect the mail. Andi Wissot labeled one basket "Mail to deliver by USPS," another basket "Mail to deliver at PS 29," and a final basket "Mail to deliver at home" (see Figure 2.2).

Launching Your Unit

At the start of any unit of study, you'll want to think of a minilesson or two, perhaps even a daylong activity that will rally your children into the big work of the whole unit. You might

Dear Families,

Students will write lots of letters this month in writing workshop as part of our persuasive letter writing unit of study. They will search for problems to solve and choose audiences to address. They will draft, revise, and edit their letters. Finally, the letters will go out into the world. We need your help with this last part. Here are the two things you can do to help us:

▶ donate envelopes and stamps (regular first-class stamps and any size envelope would be great)
▶ help your child find addresses of family members and friends

We will provide address slips for you to fill out if your child needs to get an address from home. If you get one of these address slips from your child, please print the address so your child can recopy it onto an envelope in the next day's writing workshop. The address slip will look like the one pasted below.

Your child needs to mail a letter to: _____
The address is: _____
_____
_____

We realize some of you may not be comfortable with your child using his or her own home address as the return address on the letter. We will use the school's address as the return address for each letter we mail.

Finally, we hope you will enjoy receiving these persuasive letters yourself. In years past, students have written to their parents to try to persuade them to agree to a later bedtime, to thank them for packing the best snack, or just to say "I love you." We hope you will treasure each one of the letters your child writes to you, and we hope you write back to each one.

Sincerely,

Ms. Picard Taylor

FIG. 2.1 *Sample Family Letter and Form for Addresses* Note: This figure is also available on the www.firsthand.heinemann.com website in a larger format.

FIG. 2.2 *Post Office Center in Andi's Classroom*

find yourself tempted to devote the first day of a unit to teaching children four ways to plan a letter or how to write the perfect greeting at the top of the letter, but this is a mistake. Day one needs to kick off the whole unit. And just as it is easier for a person to assemble a puzzle if the person has seen the picture on the box, so, too, it will be easier for you to teach and for your kids to participate in a unit of study if you begin the unit by teaching the big picture of the entire unit.

Using Literature to Launch the Unit

Some teachers with whom I have worked closely have chosen to read aloud an absolutely charming, funny, endearing book, *Click, Clack, Moo* (Cronin 2001), in order to launch the unit. This is the story of a farmyard full of animals who decide that they are being mistreated and write letters of protest to the farmer, who in the end gives in to their demands. One teacher I know read this book aloud and, after a rousing discussion of the book, told her children it was time for writing. "I was going to suggest that we continue writing stories for this coming month, but this book is giving me an idea," she said. "What if we do what those animals did? What if we use letter writing to change the world? If those animals did it, I'm thinking that maybe, just maybe, we could do it, too. Would you be willing to try?"

The teacher then reread *Click Clack Moo* one more time, and this time the whole class listened to the book thinking, "How can we use letter writing as a way to make the world a better place like those animals do?" The children came up with lots of ideas, and one of them was that they'd need to think about what wasn't right, what needed changing. And they were launched! Here are some other pieces of children's literature you could use to launch this study:

Picture Books with Letter Writing as Part of the Story

The Gardener, by Sarah Stewart (2007)

I Wanna Iguana, by Karen Kaufman Orloff (2004)

Dear Mr. Blueberry, by Simon James (1996)

Dear Annie, by Judith Caseley (1994)

Dear Juno, by Soyung Pak (2001)

The Jolly Pocket Postman, by Janet Ahlberg and Allan Ahlberg (1999)

Using Observation to Launch a Unit

In real life, most of us do not sit down at the desk with the intention to write someone a persuasive letter about something. Instead, we generally go about our lives, and then in the midst of doing our business, we see something that needs to be addressed. Someone is being treated unfairly, some job that needs to be done has been left undone, some opportunity needs to be seized. The question becomes, then, How can we help children go about *their* lives seeing needs that deserve to be addressed, jobs that have been left undone, and thinking, "I could write about that!"?

Many teachers find that the easiest way to help children become accustomed to generating ideas for persuasive letters they might someday write is to say, "What I want to teach you today is that writers do not usually sit at our desks and think, 'What persuasive letters might I write?' Instead, we go through our lives, paying attention to what we see and thinking, 'How could this be even better?' Then when we get an idea for a letter we could perhaps write, we jot it in a notepad."

That lesson can lead to a class full of youngsters setting forth on a walk through the school or the neighborhood, each child with a tiny notepad hanging like a necklace, and each child ready to see not only what *is* but what *could be*. Teachers can channel different students to look for certain things as they walk the halls and sidewalks. Students will generate ideas when they are given the lens to write persuasively.

Launching the Unit: An Example

"Writers," second-grade teacher Gina Braun said, "you said you wanted to write the kind of letters that will make a difference in the world, the kind of letters that will persuade or convince people to do the things we want them to do. Well, today we have a big job to do! Today, we are going to spend just a few minutes taking a close look at our lives and the lives of others at Horizon School and finding things that need to be changed. We will ask ourselves questions writers ask: 'What do I care about? What do I notice? Whom can I help?'"

Gina explained how to use the homemade tiny necklace notepads (Calkins refers to these Tiny Topics Notepads) to gather ideas on the run. She lined up her eager second graders and reminded them to move quietly in the hallway.

The quiet line of researchers rounded the first corner and a group of fourth graders made a loud entrance. The bigger-bodied fourth graders accidentally knocked into the child at the front of Gina's line.

"Whoa, whoa, whoa," said JJ, one of Gina's second graders. He immediately put his notepad against the wall to jot down the problem. "Loud, big kids in the hallway are a problem." The rest of Gina's students took note of JJ's ability to observe closely, and they were off to find more problems.

In the school library, Gina's kids noticed small piles of books off the shelves. They hypothesized that students had taken them from the shelves and then just left them sitting on the floor. A few children jotted this on their notepads.

As the students gathered more notes, Gina gave them questions to ask others during the walk:

Questions to Ask When Interviewing People Around the School

▶ Do you have problems we could help you solve?
▶ Are there things that happen here often that you want to change?
▶ What can we do to help?

As Gina's class rounded the corner to return to class, Steve Mulich, a third-grade teacher, walked by the line of researchers with notepads around their necks and pencils behind their ears. "We are looking for problems to solve, Mr. Mulich," they said.

"Oh . . . well, you should come into my classroom and look around. You may find some problems there," he replied. The researchers, once timid to walk down the hall, briskly walked into Steve's empty classroom. They peeked under tables and checked the pencil cups. They walked over to the windows in order to get a bigger view of the classroom.

"Mr. Mulich," Zoey said, "you need some comfy chairs for reading workshop. You don't have any cozy nooks. That's a problem."

"Yep, and I think you need someone to keep the pencils sharpened in the sharpened-pencils cup," said Lexi.

After you and your class have walked through a bit of the hall, collecting ideas for persuasive letters, you will want to waste no time before inviting children to write those letters. Don't worry about preteaching the greeting or anything else. Just say to children, "I've left some paper at the center of your table. Why don't you get started writing one of those letters that you've imagined writing?"

When Gina's students returned to their own classroom, they could not help but whisper a bit to the person next to them in line. They were excited about their new writing projects; they were excited to be the people in charge of changing the minds of their readers. The persuasion had begun. Gina's students soon emptied the trays of stationery. Gina helped her students see that writers live in a way where they not only see what is but also envision possibility. Her students were forever changed. From this day forward, when they saw a problem, they thought, "Maybe I could write a letter that might make the world a better place."

The First Few Days

Any one day's minilesson will always be designed to teach writers a strategy that they can use with independence from that day on. When children leave the classroom for lunch or recess, art class or to go home, you will definitely want to remind them to live their lives differently because they are now writers of persuasive letters. Tell them, "Wherever you go, whatever you do, think, 'How could I use writing to make the world a better place?'" Encourage children to wear their Tiny Topics Notepads or to carry these in their pockets and to jot ideas down. Within another day or two, you'll want to teach children that actually, a person need not physically walk through the world in order to let things spark ideas. We can, in fact, sit at our desk and pretend that we are, for example, going into the cafeteria, wearing our Tiny Topics Notepad. And while still sitting at our desk, we can think, "What ideas for persuasive writing will come to me when I am in the cafeteria?" (By the way, I'm deliberately suggesting that you use the cafeteria to illustrate your point because there are not many children who don't have some ideas for how the lunch food could be better!)

During the first days of this unit, you'll find that children crank out lots of less-than-ideal letters, reminding you of how they did similar work early in other units you've taught. The only difference is that their pieces for those units weren't written to be mailed, to be delivered. Those less-than-ideal stories could accumulate in children's folders until you got around to teaching children to revise their stories and to write better ones, and then only the best stories would be sent to readers.

You will decide whether you care terribly that some of the early letters that your children write are less than ideal. If the notion that some of those letters will leave the confines of your room before being revised bothers you, then suggest that children put their outgoing mail into a special basket and tell them that in a few days, you and they can make sure the basket of letters is delivered. Meanwhile, before delivery day, you can start intervening to show children ways to improve their letters.

Lifting the Level of Your Children's Persuasive Letters

Once your children are all writing up a storm, cranking out their little persuasive letters, you'll want to think about which skills are so important that you want to teach them right away, and then you'll want to think of how you can go about teaching those skills.

Minilesson Idea: Providing Reasons in Order to Persuade

You may want to point out to children that what they're doing in their persuasive letters is asking a favor or suggesting a solution. You'll probably want to teach children that, if they want to get their way, it helps to provide reasons to convince people.

There are lots of ways in which you could teach this. On perhaps the third day of your unit, you might begin your mini-lesson by saying, "Writers, you all are definitely living your lives differently, coming up with so many important ideas for letters that you want to write. Oscar came to school suggesting that he is going to write the janitors, asking if they can put more paper towels in the bathroom dispenser. And lots of you have other great ideas in your Tiny Topics Notepads. I'm amazed at how quickly you all have learned to come up with ideas for letters that could change the world."

You might say, "Your ideas are so important that today, we need to plan ways to write your letters so people *really* listen to you. And what I want to teach you is this: in order to make your case, you need to really talk up your idea and give lots of reasons."

Then you could demonstrate by working on your own persuasive letter in front of the children. For example, "Today I will write a letter to Mr. Olsen to ask if you all could make letter writing stationery in art class because we really need some nice paper." Be sure to remind children of the point of your lesson. "Watch how I write this letter, and notice that I'm going to say my big point (with a 'please'!) and I'm going to give lots of reasons."

Then you could pick up the marker pen, turn to the chart paper, and say, "I already started the letter." Then you could read the opening: "Dear Mr. Olsen, During art, could Class 203 have permission to make writing paper instead of placemats?" Then you could add, "Now I want to give reasons," and picking up your marker, you could write "This is important because we are writing letters that we're going to mail and we need nice paper. It is also important because our letters could make the school better." Then simply repeat what you hope children have learned and set them up to practice this work. "So, writers, do you see that when I want to write a letter that I hope will change the world, I first say what I want and then I say a reason or two why this is important?"

Then you might ask children to try it before they work on their own. It could go like this: "Let's try it. Turn to your partner and pretend you are writing a letter to your parent, asking for a pet. A horse? OK, go, 'Dear Mom and Dad, I'm writing to ask you if I . . . ,' and keep going and include a reason or two."

As you teach children to lift the level of their persuasive letter writing, you'll want to be sure to create a written record of the tips you convey to them so that children continue to draw on these throughout the unit and beyond. For example, you may start one chart titled "Making Your Letters Powerful," and one item could be "Write what you want, then write reasons why this is important."

Minilesson Idea: Using Ministories as Reasons

You'll want to think of other ways to help children make their persuasive letters more powerful. One way to be especially convincing is to tell a story of one particular incident that makes the writer's case. (See Figure 2.3.)

If you can help one of your children to do as Alexandra has done, writing the story of a small moment to illustrate her

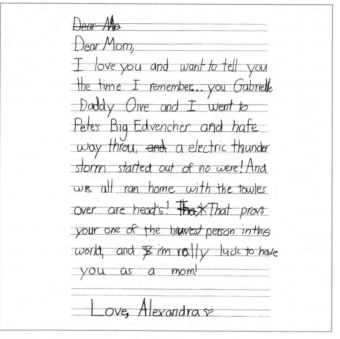

FIG. 2.3 *Alexandra's Letter to Her Mom*

point, then you'll be able to use the student's work within the teaching component of your minilesson. In a minilesson around Alexandra's work, for example, you could say, "So, writers, let me show you what Alexandra did. She'd already written, 'Dear Mom, I love you . . .' She could have listed her reasons, saying, 'I love you because . . .' But instead of writing a list of reasons, Alexandra decided to write the story of one specific small moment when her mom was particularly special."

If you want to set children up to talk about the techniques Alexandra used that they could use as well, you might say, "Watch closely for what Alexandra did that you could do, and in a minute, you'll have a chance to talk about this with your partner." Then, shifting, you could say, "Alexandra wrote, 'I remember . . . you, Gabrielle, Daddy, Olive, and I went to Pete's Big Adventure and halfway through, an electric thunderstorm started out of nowhere! And we all ran home with the towels over our heads!' Then, writers, Alexandra did something especially smart. She talked about how that small moment showed whatever it was she was trying to say. She wrote, 'That proves you're one of the bravest persons in the world, and I'm really lucky to have you as a mom!'"

For the active involvement section of that minilesson, you might simply say to children, "Would you tell each other what Alexandra did that you could do as well in your own writing?" In time, you could teach children that they can use focused anecdotes at different places in a persuasive letter. For example, a writer might want to use a small moment to illustrate the problem. Andrew wrote to the school principal, "Dear Ms. Joy, Please can you fix the water fountain." Then he used a small-moment story to illustrate the problem. "Today I tried to get a drink. I pushed the button and opened my mouth. The water went all over my face and my shirt. I saw the problem. There is gum stuck in the hole so it goes funny."

Minilesson Idea: Planning for Persuading

Although some of your minilessons will aim to teach youngsters to write in persuasive ways, citing reasons and using anecdotes to make a point, other minilessons will need to remind children that before they write persuasive letters, they need to plan for them.

To design these lessons, you'll need to think about the sorts of rehearsal and planning that might make sense for little children when writing letters. For example, you could teach children to rehearse by taking hold of a piece of letter paper, then touching the top of the page and saying aloud the greeting, and then touching the place where the letter will begin and saying aloud the start of the letter—and in persuasive letters, this will usually be the place where the writer states her claim, expresses an opinion. Then the writers can touch subsequent sections of the paper, showing either where the writer will give a reason or where she'll write, "This is important because, for example, one day . . . ," and then tell a story to convince her reader. Of course, just as partners tell stories to each other during narrative writing units, partners can rehearse the letters they plan to write with each other.

Minilesson Idea: Using Transitional Phrases

Some teachers find that giving children a few transitional phrases helps them make the transition from the claim section of a letter to the reasons. For example, some teachers teach youngsters that writers use phrases such as these to help them shift between making a claim and providing reasons:

This is important because . . .
Another reason is . . .

For example, one day . . .

This shows that . . .

Minilesson Idea: Revising Persuasive Letters

As soon as students have written one or two letters, you'll need to teach them strategies for revising and editing those letters. You might, for example, teach a minilesson that begins like this: "Writers, you all have been writing up a storm. Can you give me a thumbs-up if you have already written two letters? Three? Four?" Then you can say, "Many of you have written several letters already, and that is great. Today I want to remind you that writers don't just plan for our writing, and we don't just write our writing; we also revise our writing. Earlier this year, you revised your small-moment stories, and I want to remind you that whenever writers are writing something important, we revise. And specifically, I want to teach you that writers revise in order to make sure that our writing . . ." Then you can choose whatever quality of good writing you want to teach.

Across the unit, you will probably teach children that writers revise to make sure our writing is as detailed as it can be. For example, Alexandra's letter (in Figure 2.3) works because Alexandra does not just say, "We were at the amusement park and when it stormed, we went home." Instead, Alexandra makes her family come to life by saying that they ran home with the towels over their heads. That detail allows the reader to create a vivid image, and therefore makes the writing more persuasive.

If you teach children the importance of revising to add details, then children can practice doing this by rereading all the letters they've written so far, trying to add details to any or all of these letters. Of course, if you want to do so, you can later teach children that some details make the point, and others distract from it.

Usually you will find that anything you teach creates its own new problems. So if you encourage children to write with details, some of them will choose details that are totally obvious, and these will tend to be ineffective. For example, if a child writes, "I think vacations at the beach are the very best. We should do that more. The beach is good because it is sandy and warm," the student has chosen to describe the beach using details that are not at all surprising. How much better the writing would be if the child had written, "The beach is good because at the edge of the water, there is a line of rough and jagged rocks and I need you there to hold my hand."

The second example works not only because the writer has used details, even surprising details, but also because the writer has reached for precise words to show what he wants to show. The phrase "rough and jagged rocks" is the result of a writer trying to name exactly what he has seen. The writer could have written in a less exact way, saying, "The line is made of rocks." How much better the writing is because the writer reached past the obvious word for the precisely right word. You will probably want to teach your children to do likewise. Specifically, you can teach students to picture exactly what it is they are trying to say and then to reach for the just-right words that capture that content. Teach children that often this means thinking, "What exactly did I hear? Touch? Feel?"

All the techniques and strategies you decide to teach will need to be displayed on chart paper, and every day at the end of the minilesson, when you disperse children to work on their writing, you'll want to remind them of all the various things they have learned that they can now draw upon as needed. On any one day, some children will be starting yet another letter, others will be trying to clarify their argument, still others will be listing reasons or writing a small-moment story to illustrate their point. Some children will be rehearsing for the letter they are about to write, and others will be rereading the letter they've just completed.

Minilesson Idea: Imagining Audiences

You'll probably want each child to have a partner with whom to confer. Gather your students and show them how you and a student partner switch letters and then take turns carefully reading the other person's letter out loud. Teach students to read each letter carefully and ask, "Does my partner's letter make sense or is there something that I do not understand?" Writers can meanwhile observe as the other person reads their draft, noticing the reader's perplexity, laughter, or concern. Writers can ask themselves, "Did my letter make the reader feel something?" When a writer has the chance to learn from someone's response to a draft, this will often prompt revision. Writers will often change some words so the letter makes more sense or helps the reader experience a bigger feeling.

We can also teach writers that they can step into the role of reader, rereading their own drafts as if seeing them for the first time.

You might encourage readers to imagine their own audiences in this way: "Children, try closing your eyes and picture your reader reading your letter. Picture her face. Picture her body. Where do you want your reader to laugh aloud or to feel something? Will the reader feel as you hope he or she feels? Could you add something to your letter that will affect your reader?"

Picturing the audience will make writers aware that their every word will be read by someone close to them. They'll know their words matter.

When you help children think of their audience, they become deeply invested in their writing. Once, at the end of the workshop, Oscar called my name. "Sarah! Sarah! I messed up. Something is not right!" He was worried. I could see it on his face. I looked down at his paper and noticed he was writing to Karl.

"You want it to make sense for Karl, don't you?" I asked. He nodded his head. "Oscar, take the time now to reread and make the changes. You can do it. You can make it make sense for Karl. He will be able to understand it." Oscar cared so much about his writing because of his attention to audience. (See Figure 2.4.)

It is easy to see how partners can help one another focus on audience—they can be that audience! Following are some other ways writing partners can help one another during writing workshop.

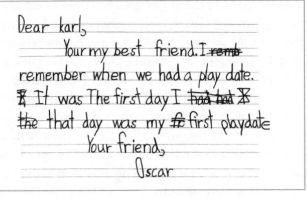

> Dear karl,
>   Your my best friend. I ~~remb~~
> remember when we had a play date.
> ~~It~~ It was The first day I ~~had had It~~
> ~~the~~ that day was my ~~fir~~ first playdate
>   Your friend,
>   Oscar

FIG. 2.4 *Oscar's Letter to Karl About Their First Play Date*

A writing partner can:

▶ Read the draft of a letter aloud to the writer so the writer has a chance to listen to his or her writing, thinking "Does this sound right?"

▶ Read the draft of a letter and point out a great section of the letter and suggest ways the writer can add on to the best parts of the letter.

Minilesson Idea: Using a Word Wall to Spell Conventionally

When students like those in Oscar's class worried that they did not "make it right," my colleagues and I asked ourselves, "What do *we* expect the students to get right?" Teachers cannot hold first graders accountable to spell words correctly that we have not taught. However, we can hold students accountable for spelling the high-frequency words that we've taught. Many first- and second-grade teachers use a word wall in their classrooms to store these high-frequency words (Cunningham and Hall 2001). A word wall is usually in an accessible place so children can refer to it often, and students use the word wall throughout the year. You most likely taught your students to use this as a spelling tool in a previous unit, but if you have not drawn students' attention to the expanding wall of spelling resources in a while, this is a worthwhile minilesson to teach inside this unit of study. Because the students are so completely wrapped up in the urgency of sending their letters out to a real audience, they vigorously use the word wall to fix spelling mistakes. For this unit, you might include on your word wall some possible greeting and closing words for letters (to see a photo of word wall, go to our website, www.firsthand.heinemann.com).

When gathering children for a minilesson that reminds them to use the word wall to help fix spelling mistakes, we need to remember to be explicit. We cannot simply say, "Check the word wall," without teaching the students *how* to check the word wall. We can demonstrate how a writer rereads a persuasive letter and looks carefully for words that do not look right. You may do this by reading each word one by one out loud and saying, "Yes, aha, that looks right," and then pausing when you get to a high-frequency word you realize is not spelled correctly. Then say to the students, "This looks wrong. Wait! I think this word is on the word wall. I know it begins with a *w* and *w* is at the end of the alphabet, so let me find the *w* on the wall and read all the words in that section." You may walk over to the wall, search for the *w* section, pointing to it. Then you can read each of the words under that letter, searching for the exact one you need.

You may decide to get the students involved during the active engagement part of the lesson by asking them to reread a draft of one of their letters, checking that they've spelled word wall words correctly. Alternatively, you may ask them to help you continue rereading the draft of your letter, written on large chart paper, helping you check that you've spelled as well as possible. Of course, in such a situation you will have made an error or two, allowing children to spot your errors and to rectify them. Regardless of what you choose, you will need to scoot around the meeting area during this active engagement and remind the students of how they can use the word wall as a resource. Show them that they can isolate the sound at the start of the word, find the letter that marks that sound on the word wall, and proceed from there.

Finally, the students' letters will be ready! Chapter 4 describes the ways you can organize your students to put their letters out into the world.

CHAPTER THREE

Writing Persuasive Reviews

Christopher had written about the day he went to a movie. This was clearly an important writing project to him. I leaned in to read his draft. His narrative retold scene after scene from the movie. It was a personal narrative but there was no personal story in the draft.

Reading Christopher's draft, I was tempted to suggest that instead of retelling the movie, he might consider writing about his experience. Was there one particular part of the evening that mattered especially to him? Trying to channel him in this direction, I asked, "Christopher, why are you writing this?"

"It was so great! Spider-Man was flying all around, chasing the bad guys. . . ."

And so I made my choice. Christopher did not want to tell the story of sharing popcorn with his brother. He wanted to shout from the second-grade hallway, "Everybody, go and see *Spider-Man!*" I made the decision that he wanted to write a review and that I could help him do so. Since then, my colleagues and I in the Teachers College Reading and Writing Project have decided to help all youngsters explore this genre.

Many of us have students like Christopher who want to write about the movies they have seen, the books they have read, the video games they have played, and the food they have enjoyed. Youngsters are eager for the chance to participate in a unit of study that can help them write movie, book, food, and, yes, even video game reviews.

This chapter provides an overview of how a unit on writing reviews could unfold. This particular unit is designed to help children develop the muscles that are essential in persuasive writing. If during one year, your school introduces children to persuasive writing by teaching them to write persuasive letters, the following year, your school might revisit persuasive writing, this time through a unit of study on review writing. Perhaps children could write persuasive literary essays the following year.

Preparing for the Unit with Conversations

Before this unit begins, give your children lots of opportunities to express their opinions and talk persuasively. Pause during read-alouds to solicit opinions. If you've been reading Cynthia Rylant's *Gooseberry Park* (2007), you might say, "What do you think about Kona?" Perhaps one child might say he thinks Kona is brave. Another youngster might blurt in, "But I think Murray the bat is braver! He is hiding out in a house to babysit the baby squirrels. That takes bravery!" Take these opinions seriously and ask children to persuade you by offering evidence to support their claims. You can ask children to be more persuasive at other times of the day, too—when a child complains the food at lunch was horrible, for example, you can ask for evidence and support. See Figure 3.1 for more ideas on preparing for writing reviews.

Develop ideas for book and movie reviews through conversations about:

- ▶ children's reactions to characters, authors, or genres
- ▶ comparisons between one version and another of a book or movie

Develop ideas for video game reviews through conversations about:

- ▶ the comparison of a new version and older version of the same game
- ▶ the quality of the graphic images

Develop ideas for food or restaurant reviews through conversations about:

- ▶ children's judgments of taste, texture, smell, appearance of food, service, and atmosphere
- ▶ comparisons of restaurants that are similar in some ways

FIG. 3.1 *Some Possible Ways to Generate Ideas for This Unit*

Unit Materials and Paper

As you approach a unit of study on writing reviews, you will want to read selected reviews aloud to your children. It will be especially helpful if you read reviews of books, movies, and places that children know well, because this can help children see what is (and also what is not) included in a review. Children can look at published book or movie reviews and discern the qualities of writing that make it interesting for the reader, just as they have done with other mentor texts. A few websites featuring reviews are listed in Figure 3.2.

Invite children to sort and study reviews. Have conversations about what each kind of review tends to contain. As a class, you'll probably discover that reviews for books and movies usually include descriptions of characters, setting, and plot, along with opinions about the authors or actors and directors. Reviews about restaurants and food tend to include descriptions of the service, prices, atmosphere, taste, and appearance of the food—the entire dining experience. Writers of these reviews even include descriptions such as "I was greeted at the door by a cheerful hostess." Video game reviews often compare newer game versions with previous versions, describing graphics, trick moves, and whether it is easy to progress through the levels.

Invite children to talk about their observations of reviews. They'll probably notice that reviewers often talk directly to readers saying, "You will love . . ." They may notice spicy language. Is the movie thrilling? A chiller? They will probably notice that reviewers sometimes include advice, "Arrive early . . ." or "Skip this one."

www.commonsensemedia.org. This site contains reviews
for books, movies, and video games. Most reviews
are written by adults, but there are brief reviews written by students.

www.pbskids.org/readingrainbow/books. This site contains
audio-recorded reviews. Students can visit the site
and listen to reviews of hundreds of books, some of
them written and spoken by students.

www.cyberkids.com. This site has movie and book reviews
written by students.

www.kidreviewer.com. This site is authored by a student.
He reviews movies and video games. He also dis-
plays a blog.

www.kidsfirst.org. This site has short (4–6 sentence) film
reviews written by adults and students.

Information on these sites changes rapidly. Teachers
should read the information at each site before inviting
students to look at the sites independently.

FIG. 3.2 *Websites Offering Potential Persuasive Reviews to Use as
Mentor Texts*

You will also want to try your hand at review writing!
Consider writing and posting a review of a book on
Amazon.com or Barnesandnoble.com. Your children will be
delighted to see your review online. You'll find that writing a
review can be complicated and this will help you discern the

teaching that you will need to do in this unit of study. There are two sample teacher-written reviews available through a link accompanying the listing of this book on the www.heinemann.com website.

You will want to place copies of your reviews alongside the other reviews you collect. You may want to make copies of selected reviews so that your children can keep these reviews on hand as they write. Throughout the course of the unit, students will revisit these mentor reviews, seeking specific craft moves to emulate.

Finally, before you begin the unit, you will probably want to think about the sorts of paper you can imagine providing your children. Do you imagine the reviews will be written on single sheets of paper? Do you imagine they'll be written in small booklets like those you may have provided when students wrote stories? There is probably no one answer to that question. The teachers in schools in which I work have tended to channel children toward writing each of their reviews within a small booklet, and we tell children these are similar to the booklets real critics sometimes carry into restaurants or movies when they are collecting information for a review. The youngsters plan their reviews by touching the pages of the review booklets and rehearsing their persuasive reviews aloud. They sometimes use the ideas in the chart in Figure 3.1 to help them rehearse and then draft their reviews.

Launching Your Unit

Remember that the lead in a unit of study, like the lead in a piece of writing, must invite people to come along on a journey. Your lead to this unit will need to build a drumroll for the unit, evoking a heightened anticipation for what is to come. We have launched the unit by sharing a review of a familiar text—say, the latest *Judy Moody* book—and then involving the entire class in a conversation about the power that reviews have in the real world. We've read aloud a variety of reviews, including one of a television show, a film, and a restaurant. Then we have invited children to join in this kind of writing: "Is there any way *you* might have the courage to become reviewers, for real, writing about books and movies and maybe even games and then sending your reviews out into the world?"

Of course, this is not the only way to launch a unit on reviews. You could, for example, decide instead to open the unit by inviting a local restaurant or movie critic to your classroom. The critic might tell stories about dressing in disguise when she goes into restaurants, then collecting notes in her special steno notebook. She might add that she uses the two columns in the steno notebook for distinctly different purposes. One column might be for her to write the things she notices and the other, for opinions and thoughts. Children can try this too!

Sample of the Kinds of Notes Critics Might Write

Crumbs Bakery

- Smells good when you walk inside

- Music—fun, upbeat

- Cupcakes look good! So many displayed at once! Colorful

- Staff helps me pick out the best ones

- They pack them in a safe little box with a colored sticker.

- Cupcakes are sweet, moist. Frosting is not too thick. Also, not too sugary. (Some places have frosting where you can feel the grains of the sugar. I don't like that. I like smooth frosting.)

- There are a few tables to sit and eat your cupcake if you do not want to take it to go with you.

- It's close to the subway—easy to get to.

Suggest that for homework, children live like reviewers, paying attention and forming persuasive opinions whenever they go to a restaurant, watch a television show, play a computer game. You might give your children steno notepads or "reviewer's notebooks" to use at home, and you might teach them that even when they are not in the writing workshop, they can be thinking about the reviews they want to write and collecting ideas for what they will say to persuade people of of their opinion. Sometimes, my colleagues and I have found that the easiest way to evoke excitement is by giving children a new tool, one that represents the work of the upcoming unit. The notebooks themselves can help rev up children's enthusiasm for the unit, and children will love them even more if you suggest that for homework, they paste pictures onto the covers that represent texts and places they could review. After students do this, ask questions such as, "*Which* Henry and Mudge book might you review?" and "Who would read your review, and where would they find it?" and "How will you persuade them to believe you?"

In the classroom, tell children, "Go to it." Provide children with whatever paper choice you decided on prior to the unit—perhaps little booklets—and fill paper trays with paper. Teach children that they can rehearse for these reviews by touching the part of the paper on which they will write and saying aloud the words they want to write. First a child can say his opinion, then he can provide reasons for that opinion.

Let children start writing reviews to their hearts' content, and as they work with zeal on this project, you can see what they understand about the genre. If you see children stating their opinion early in the review, support this decision. You can say, "It is really smart of you to realize that reviewers often state an idea, opinion about a movie, a book, or a restaurant. And you have done that! This is a smart decision."

As you confer, look for children who have had a hard time coming out and stating an opinion. Some children may ramble, offering assorted comments about their subject. Teach these writers that in order to write a review, the writer needs to know what she wants to say. It helps for a child to ask herself, "How do I *really* feel about this book (this movie, this meal)?"

Lifting the Level of Students' Persuasive Reviews

Once children have started writing, you can dive in and coach them on some ways to make their reviews even stronger.

Minilesson Idea: Elaborating Within Your Review

Many children will need you to remind them that details matter more than almost anything else. Children's first attempts at reviews will not contain a lot of elaboration; expect this, and know that the good thing is this leaves you lots of room to teach! In conferences, help a writer see that instead of writing, "When you walk in, you will see cupcakes," he could write, "When you walk in, you will see three shelves of cupcakes and they'll come in all the colors of the rainbow. You will smell the sweet, warm smell of newly baked cupcakes."

As they work on elaborations, you will also want to teach your children that a reviewer states an opinion, and then gives reasons. You may want to hold up your fist when you say, "We say our opinion," and then hold up one finger, another, and another as you refer to the list of supporting evidence. Of course, you'll refer to your own writing as a case in point. In one minilesson, I said to the children, "After I write my opinion—that Crumbs is the best bakery for cupcakes—I need to give some reasons that support my opinion, or I won't persuade anyone!" Holding up my fingers as I continued, I listed my reasons across my fingers. "Crumbs is the best bakery in my neighborhood because they have a beautiful display of all their cupcakes so you can see what is available. The people who work at Crumbs are always friendly. Another reason Crumbs is the best bakery is that the cupcakes are sweet but not too sweet, with the perfect amount of frosting, about a half of an inch!" Of course, instead of sharing your review, you could share one written by a child.

Children may need support thinking of what they can say about a book, a restaurant, a movie, or a game. This is a perfect opportunity to revisit the mentor text of the unit. You can remind them that the mentor text taught them that in a *food* review, a reviewer can describe the setting of the restaurant, the food itself, or the service she received. In a *book* review, a reviewer can describe the characters, the special features, the ways the book is like or unlike others. For a *movie* review, a reviewer can describe not only the characters but also the actors who play those characters. For a *video game* review, the writer can describe the graphics, the enjoyment level, and the amount of reading a player needs to do in order to play. Hopefully, you'll have children writing all these kinds of reviews. If you teach them that they can study mentor texts for ideas about the content of their own reviews, that one lesson on mentor text can be applicable to all the reviews your children are writing.

You can also help students elaborate on their opinions by citing direct quotes from other people. Say to the writers, "You can be even more convincing if you find and use direct quotes from the characters, chefs, diners, or players. You can hunt around for the things people say about the food at the restaurant. Similarly, you can hunt for things the characters say in books or games. You can record what your friends say about the movie, book, or game. Direct quotes will enliven a review." For a restaurant review, writers may write, "Three diners at the table near me said that lunch at the American Girl Place is 'the best birthday present ever.'" For a video game review, writers may write, "When you win a game, the character Slash sometimes says, 'You *rock*!'"

My colleagues and I show the students how to elaborate by demonstrating the process of doing this. I recently showed a class of first graders that after I wrote my opinion about the video game Guitar Hero III, I thought, "Why exactly do I enjoy this game?" and then I wrote, "When you play the song and miss too many notes, you can get booed off the stage. Some people may think it is embarrassing, but I think it is a funny feature. Whenever it happens, my brother Andy says, 'Uh-oh, you gotta do it again.'"

Then I suggest children take out one of their reviews, rereading to think, "Where could I add a direct quote to support my opinion?"

As students continue drafting their reviews, they will learn new strategies for improving their reviews and will revise to incorporate their new knowledge into reviews they wrote earlier. Each time you teach a new strategy for making a review even better, children can comb through their drafts of reviews, using the new strategy to prompt revisions. (See Figure 3.3 for an example of revision.)

Minilesson Idea: Writing Catchy Leads

You will probably want to show children some ways in which they can start a review in a sparky, catchy way. In a minilesson, I showed children that I tried several leads for my restaurant review.

- "This is the best vanilla cupcake I ever had," said a little boy sitting at the table next to me at Crumbs bakery on the Upper West Side. I agreed.

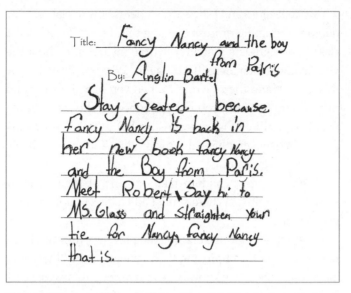

Page 1: Stay seated because Fancy Nancy is back in her new book fancy Nancy and the Boy from Paris. Meet Robert, say hi to Ms. Glass and straighten your tie for Nancy, fancy Nancy, that is.

FIG. 3.3 *Review That Shows a Student Trying Out Various Elaboration Techniques*

▶ Ben and Jerry's is famous for ice cream, Starbucks for coffee, and in my part of New York City, Crumbs is famous for cupcakes.

▶ I love cupcakes and I eat several every day. So trust me when I say Crumbs is the best place in New York City for cupcakes!

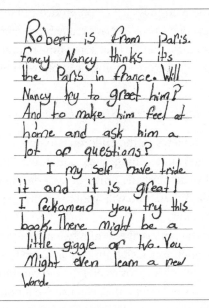

Page 2: Robert is from Paris. fancy Nancy thinks it's the Paris in france. Will Nancy try to greet him? And to make him feel at home and ask him a lot of questions? I my self have tride it and it is great! I reckamend you try this book. There might be a little giggle or two. You Might even learn a new Word.

FIG. 3.3 (*continued*)

After showing my leads, I talked about some of the different techniques I tried—techniques that could be used in any kind of review. "A reviewer can start with a quote (it could be) from a character, reader, author, or customer. Alternately, a reviewer can start by forwarding an opinion. Then, too, the lead can illustrate the reviewer's credibility. Give them all a try!"

Over time, you may use a conference to help one writer see that many of his reviews have really brash beginnings, and you might suggest that he take some time to build a relationship with readers before coming right out with his opinion.

Minilesson Idea: Writing Strong Endings

By now, the reviews in the children's folders will be getting better through your teaching. The students will be writing with zeal and pleasure, but they may be wondering how to end their reviews. Perhaps you will want to teach a minilesson that attends to endings.

Much of the persuasive writing we are exposed to in our culture has repetition. Catchphrases are used to sell products in print and television commercials. We can teach our students that in a similar way, they can use repetition to their advantage when they write their persuasive reviews. "Critics, I have been thinking long and hard about how to end my review of Crumbs bakery. So last night I was up late searching for a perfect way to end my review. It came to me as I was watching commercials. The little song for one of the commercials was stuck in my head, and then I realized something. One reason the song stuck with me is because the words just kept repeating. It got me thinking about our reviews. If we want our reviews to be persuasive, we could repeat our opinion at the end! We can just simply say the same thing again."

"I also noticed that commercials sometimes end with a rating. We can invent a rating system we'll use often as a reviewer. Remember the newspaper critic who uses stars?

We could try that—giving something three out of five stars, hearts, balloons, or whatever. Here, let me try that with my review so you can see how it goes for me. . . ."

Minilesson Idea: Learning from Mentor Texts

As students revise, you may want to invite them to reread mentor reviews carefully, this time reading them not as first-time readers who want to understand the author's message, but instead as writers who want to notice the author's craft. A reader might notice the interesting word choices the author has made for example. Teach your students to pause at sections of the review they like and to think, "What did the writer do that works?"

You may use other guiding questions:

- What is interesting about this review?
- How does the writer start and end the review?
- What part of the book, food, restaurant, game, or movie does the writer actually write about?

When you demonstrate how to read mentor texts, be sure you point to the thing the author has done that you like, name it, and then imagine a place in your own writing where you could try that same writing move. For example, many movie and video game reviews contain sentences such as "This movie was made to entertain children but it also entertains adults." You might read a line like that in a mentor text aloud and say, "Hmm . . . I think that sentence right there is important. I think it is important for a reviewer to say who would appreciate this movie, or use this video game, or eat at this restaurant. I think maybe we could call this kind of sentence something."A student of yours might shout out a name for this kind of sentence. If the children want to call it a "target audience" sentence, call it that. If they want to call it a "who's it for" sentence, go with that.

Then suggest to your students that writers often try to do a lot of things the mentor author has done. "Writers, I was thinking I could try adding a sentence to tell people who will appreciate Crumb's bakery. I might add, 'The colorful cupcakes in the window suggest this shop is for kids, but one whiff of the fresh-baked air and everyone in your home will want to have a bite of these tasty treats.'"

Remember your goal is not for all your students to add a sentence naming who will appreciate their subject. The goal is for all writers to read and reread a mentor's text, notice a few interesting things, and try some of them in their own writing. Give your students some time to reread the mentor text during the active engagement part of this minilesson. As the kids reread, move around the meeting area collecting all the things they are noticing. Jot these down somewhere because they will make helpful lists later. Figure 3.4 shows the list of things one second-grade class noticed while perusing a few mentor texts.

This minilesson will prompt some children to revise, incorporating whatever they notice from a mentor text. Others will be in the midst of writing a new review and will use lessons from this minilesson to effect their first draft reviews.

▶ Start with the basics or important information.
- Book reviews have author, illustrator, and title, names of the main characters, setting, and a basic gist of the story.
- Movie reviews have title, names of main characters and the actors who play those characters, setting, and plot, as well as locations where you can see the movie.
- Restaurant reviews have name and address of the restaurant, name of the chef, names of the things the reviewer ate. Some reviews include the price of the food and a description of the restaurant décor.
- Video game reviews have the name and version of the game, game systems on which the game can be played, a description of how the game is played, and often a description of the setting or plot or the characters in the game. Some video game reviews include tips for how to move up to higher levels.

▶ List the reasons a person may like or dislike this book, restaurant, movie, or game.
- "You may like it if you are the kind of person who . . ."
- "Only for five- or six-year-olds because . . ."
- "Grown-ups will not be happy because . . ."

▶ End with a comparison with another restaurant, movie, or game that is similar to or different from the one you reviewed.
- "If you liked this book, you may also like . . ."
- "A better option is to play . . ."

FIG. 3.4 *Things We Noticed in Reviews We Read*

Minilesson Idea: Revising with a Checklist

You'll probably want to ask all your children to choose one of the many reviews they have written and revised and prepare it to go out in the world. Chapter 4 describes exciting ways to do this. These include a school newspaper, of course, but also neighborhood walks to post the reviews in the places people will go when they are looking for advice for a restaurant, book, movie, or video game. We suggest posting at local libraries, bookstores, restaurants, and game shops.

Choosing the review or reviews the children want to put out in the world will be an exciting process. You can teach students to go back into their folders, self-assess their own writing, and choose the review(s) they want to revise, edit, and publish. You might convene students in the meeting area asking them to bring their folders full of reviews. Post a chart that includes the qualities of good reviews that you and your children noticed at the beginning of the unit. Teachers can reread the chart with the students and show the students how to compare their own reviews with the qualities on the chart. Students can begin rereading their own reviews during the minilesson and continue throughout writing time, searching for the one that contains the qualities of a strong review.

You may also want to introduce revision checklists to your students. Revision checklists are not meant to be a laundry list of items a writer checks off when she creates a new piece of writing. Rather, revision checklists can be used to help a writer remember each strategy that was taught in a unit of study. Relying on memory alone is sometimes not enough, and these simple tools can be created with your students. For sample revision checklists, see the www.firsthand.heinemann.com website.

It will be important for students to read the reviews they select slowly and carefully, self-assessing the things they have done well and the things they still need to do before putting their writing out into the world. You can help them form small strategy lesson groups to help students with similar aspirations continue reworking their chosen reviews.

Minilesson Idea: Using Comparisons to Persuade

If the first day of revision helped students select a review to revise and begin selecting sections of it that merit further work, perhaps the next revision minilesson might convey one way students might chose to make their writing more persuasive.

The students' initial drafts may contain simple sentences such as, "I think you will like this movie." Teachers can challenge their students to be more persuasive and write with a stronger persuasive voice. Students can accomplish this by using comparison to convey their true opinion. You may want to give children some language that can help them do this:

- If you liked _____ then you will love _____.

- Most kids who liked _____ also liked _____.

- If _____ is a three star _____, then this is a _____ star _____.

Students could reread their own drafts to find the places where they could use comparison to make their persuasive voices stronger.

Minilesson Idea: Editing for Capitalization of Proper Nouns

Your students will make changes to their reviews that will no doubt make them better. They will be excited to put them out in the world, but you may be worried about misspelled words, capitalization, or punctuation. It certainly will be time for you to support students' editing strategies.

In every unit, we try to grow the amount of editing work for which a young writer can be held responsible. In this unit of study, we focus on editing that seems to matter especially in reviews. This includes capitalization of proper nouns.

If your students already have an editing checklist from other units of study, it probably already includes items such as, "Reread your writing carefully to make sure capital letters are only where they belong" or "Make sure capitals are at beginnings of sentences and not in the middle words." On this day you can add the following reminders to the chart:

▶ Capitalize the first letter of people's first and last names.

▶ Capitalize the first letter of each word in a restaurant's name or a book, movie, or video game title. But don't capitalize the little words such as *and*.

In a minilesson, show children how to reread writing in search of words that need to be capitalized. Make sure some of your own writing has capitalization errors to correct! Then model for the students the process of rereading, asking yourself, "Are any of these proper nouns?" Then, when you find them, stop to capitalize them.

Invite your students to become engaged in the minilesson. They can take out their own reviews and begin the search for proper nouns to capitalize or they can help you edit your writing. Encourage them to reread slowly to find the places that need to be changed.

Christopher and his fellow review writers were excited and proud when they finished their reviews. He was excited because he was able to write about movies and video games, two of his favorite things. Christopher was proud to put his review out into the world using our class newsletter. He knew other people would read it and hopefully be persuaded by his reviews. The next time our principal came to visit the classroom, Christopher immediately led her over to the newsstand in the hallway and invited her to take a copy of the newsletter, which included his review.

The celebration for this unit of study can take on a few different forms. Chapter 4 describes some authentic ways reviews can be put out into the world and the process teachers use to set up the publication.

CHAPTER FOUR

Delivering Persuasive Writing to an Audience

All the moments of our lives should feel purposeful. Every moment of thinking, writing, creating, hypothesizing, and playing should matter.

I learned from principals and other staff developers to talk to students about purpose. One of the strongest instructional leaders I've worked with, Daria Rigney, used to visit my writing workshop and ask young writers, "Why are you working on this story?" or "Why are you choosing that specific strategy?" Later, Carl Anderson taught me to ask students, "Why are you writing this?" and "Who are you planning to give this to when you are finished?" At first, I doubted if first graders could answer these questions. Initially, I thought students wrote because it was writing time or because they were trying to impress their friends. Carl Anderson helped by nudging me to suggest audiences and purposes for the writing my students were doing.

Putting Student Writing into the World

During a persuasive writing unit of study, the walls of the classroom dissolve and student writing goes out into the world. Letters are promptly delivered to their receivers. Reviews are put in places where eager information seekers will read them. The following sections describe the organizational systems that will support teachers and students in the effort to put persuasive writing out into the world.

A System for Weekly Delivery of Letters

Instead of asking each student to collect a month's worth of letters in a folder and to then choose only one letter to send out into the world, the teachers with whom I work ask writers to select letters that will be actually mailed at the end of each week. There is a designated delivery day once each week.

Communication and organization are necessary to implement a weekly delivery system. My colleagues and I begin by putting three or four celebration dates—often Fridays—on the large class calendar. We write, "letter celebration and delivery day," so that students work toward approaching deadlines. We clearly communicate the delivery system for the letters and organize a routine for students to follow at the end of each week. Here's a sample routine:

▶ Before Friday delivery of letters, writers must:
  • Plan and draft letter.
  • Reread and revise the best you can.

- Share with your writing partner if you think you need advice.
- Take an address slip home if you need to get the address from someone in your family.
- Address an envelope and put your letter inside.
- Put the envelope in the basket that matches the method of delivery you will use.
- Use a stamp if you are sending your letter via the U.S. Postal Service (USPS).
- Use an airmail sticker or stamp if you are sending your letter to someone in a different country.

It is important to set up a delivery routine that the students can manage as the unit unfolds. Many teachers create baskets for mail to be delivered (see Figure 2.2 on page 22).

One basket may be for mail that can be delivered at school, another basket for mail that will need stamps or a simple trip home in a student's backpack.

A note of caution: The first time students address envelopes, they will be messy. All learners approximate new tasks before they implement them correctly. Although teachers accept approximations in primary-level writing workshops, the U.S. Postal Service is less accomodating. There is a specific format the writer needs to follow when addressing envelopes.

My colleagues and I have learned several ways to ease this frustration. Some teachers supply preprinted return address labels.

Editing Tips

Reread the letter and make sure it makes sense and sounds good to the reader.

Reread and listen for the ends of your sentences. Put end punctuation at the places where your sentences stop.

Reread your letter and listen for sentences you wrote that convey the urgency of the problem. End these sentences with an exclamation mark.

Reread your letter and listen for sentences you wrote that ask the reader a question. End these sentences with a question mark.

Reread your writing and look for places where you wrote the names of specific people. Use capital letters for the first letter of a person's name.

Reread your writing and look for places where you may have written a capital letter in the middle of a word. Change it to lowercase so your words are easy to read.

A writer from class 1-203
P.S. 29
425 Henry St.
New York, NY 10019

Other teachers order a class rubber stamp with a return address. Still others use peel-off labels with lines printed on them and ask students to write on those lines.

Teachers may also want to organize a delivery route and select different student postal workers for each delivery day. Sorters place all mail to be delivered by hand or to family members in each writer's classroom mailbox. You do not want a letter that should go home in Oscar's backpack to end up in the USPS mailbox without a stamp! Then the postal workers can deliver school mail to the appropriate classroom or to that teacher's mailbox.

At the end of the day, each student sending a letter through the U.S. Postal Service can carry his or her own writing while the class walks to the nearest USPS drop box or into the school's office to use the outgoing mailbox. One by one, those students can drop their letters into the mailbox (see Figure 4.1).

Posting Reviews in Public Places

Teachers show students where different kinds of writing belong in the world. It makes sense, then, for teachers to show students the places where people will go to read book, food, movie, and video game reviews.

FIG. 4.1 *Students Dropping Their Letters into the Mailbox*

Reviews are on the Internet, posted in places where books, video games, and movie tickets are bought, as well as on sites where you can book a restaurant reservation. Reviews can also be found in the restaurants, movie and game rental shops, bookstores, and libraries. These physical locations often have a special shelf with recommended titles and reviews from staff members. Restaurants often post all or part of a favorable review from a critic next to their menu in their main window or doorway. Reviews can also be found in local weekly newspapers. Some newspapers or magazines have a special dedicated page that goes out on a certain day of the week so readers learn to expect movie reviews on Fridays or book reviews on Tuesdays.

We can organize a routine to help our students put their writing out into the world in similar ways. Teachers can do this through a weekly or monthly newspaper or through trips to local bookstores, game shops, libraries, and restaurants.

Juliet Spagliardi showed her class the shelves of book recommendations at the local bookstore and library. Then she and her colleagues in the second grade at P.S. 29 called the bookstore and library managers to ask if their students could post their book reviews on a shelf. Juliet's class had their book review writing celebration at the local library (see Figure 4.2). Student posted published reviews next to the shelf where each reviewed book was displayed. Parents came along to admire the persuasive writing, and library visitors were thankful to have children's book recommendations written by children!

FIG. 4.2 *Students' Reviews Posted at the Library*

Reflecting and Celebrating at Unit's End

Students post signs, deliver letters, and possibly publish reviews of books, food, and movies each week during a persuasive writing unit. Whatever the focus of such a unit, the celebration that ends the unit inevitably feels different than other writing celebrations. Signs are already posted; letters are already delivered; reviews are already published. Some teachers therefore add on an additional step of a culminating celebration—a time to reflect on and celebrate all that this new writing has accomplished. Following are a few culminating ideas popular among teachers and their students.

Publicly Display Copies of the Original Letters Students Sent and Replies They Received

Sarah Carolan, a first-grade teacher, collected all of the replies her students received to their letters. She made a class book that held both the letters and the replies. The students used small index cards to tell the stories of why they wrote their letters and how they felt about the responses they received. The class book was displayed on a large table for visitors to read on the last day of the unit. Instead of having one large celebration, teachers who chose this option had their doors open all day long for visitors to come inside and browse the book.

Other teachers displayed photocopies of the letters and responses on a bulletin board for visitors to see. Visitors noticed qualities of persuasive writing and often wrote comments to students about their abilities to solve difficult problems.

Visitors also listened to writers talk about the changes their letters produced in the world. For example, Sam took his visitors on a tour of the school's third floor. He showed them the recycling signs he made as a result of the letter he received from his local borough president encouraging him to make a difference at his school.

Make Copies of a Class Newspaper or of Collected Reviews and Place These on a Newsstand in the Hallway

In some K–2 classrooms, many children will have worked on a similar kind of review. Reviews that belong together can be published in a single volume. Some classrooms publish their own versions of the *Zagat Guide to Restaurants*, their own *TV Guides*, or *New York Times* book reviews. Whatever volume is created, it needs to be distributed. Many classrooms make homemade newsstands so that people who pass by the classroom and also people who attend the culmination celebration can help themselves to the promotional materials.

The Road Ahead

A decade ago, one of my former students, Diana, called me from her new school. She had recently moved to a small town with her parents and younger brother. Her voice sounded urgent.

"Ms. Picard?"

"Yes, Diana. Good to hear from you!"

"Ms. Picard, can you write a letter to my teacher and tell her that I do not read baby books? She told me to read these books that are baby books. I hate them."

"Diana, she may just be giving you something easy to read at the beginning of the year. She may just want you to feel comfortable."

"No, they are baby books! Level 1.1! I told her I read level M, like Junie B. Jones, but she says I have to start at level 1.1. I want you to write her a letter and tell her I do not read baby books!"

I knew Diana understood the power of persuasion and so I suggested that she be the one to write a letter to her new teacher. "Use what you know about writing persuasive letters," I told her.

Diana was quiet for a moment. "But what evidence can I give her in my letter?" she asked, continuing her effort to lure me to be her advocate. Before Diana and I had finished talking, she'd realized she could staple a copy of her report card from second grade and a running record from her cumulative file onto her letter.

As I hung up the phone with Diana, I was amazed by the power of this girl, advocating for herself. Diana was able to stand up for herself because the groundwork for persuasive writing had been laid in her previous school experience.

Just recently, I again talked with Diana and, this time she was writing an admissions essay as part of an application to a selective high school. Diana was once again advocating for herself. In my mind, I still pictured her as the second grader sitting at our meeting area, listening intently, nodding with understanding or opening her mouth wide and cocking her head to the side when the teaching was not so clear. I pictured her rushing off to do her best work for the people she cared about most.

This unit of study helped transform the way Diana viewed herself and her world. This writing unit has helped students like Diana negotiate the world outside of the four walls of their classrooms. It is my hope that you are now thinking of the Dianas in your classroom and of the gift you can give them by teaching them to advocate for themselves.

WORKS CITED

Professional Books

Anderson, Carl. 2005. *Assessing Writers*. Portsmouth, NH: Heinemann.

Angelillo, Janet. 2003. *Writing About Reading: From Book Talk to Literary Essays, Grades 3–8*. Portsmouth, NH: Heinemann.

Bomer, Katherine, and Randy Bomer. 2001. *For a Better World: Reading and Writing for Social Action*. Portsmouth, NH: Heinemann.

Calkins, Lucy, et al. 2003. *Units of Study for Primary Writing*. 7 vols. Portsmouth, NH: Firsthand.

Cunningham, Patricia M., and Dorothy Hall. 2001. *Month by Month Phonics for First Grade*. New York: Scholastic.

Parsons, Stephanie. 2007. *Second Grade Writers: Units of Study to Help Children Focus on Audience and Purpose*. Portsmouth, NH: Heinemann.

Ray, Katie Wood. 2004. *About the Authors: Writing Workshop with Our Youngest Writers*. Portsmouth, NH: Heinemann.

Children's Books

Ahlberg, Janet, and Allan Ahlberg. 1999. *The Jolly Pocket Postman*. New York: Puffin.

Caseley, Judith. 1994. *Dear Annie*. New York: HarperTrophy.

Cronin, Doreen. 2001. *Click, Clack, Moo: Cows That Type*. New York: Scholastic.

James, Simon. 1996. *Dear Mr. Blueberry*. New York: Aladdin.

Orloff, Karen Kaufman. 2004. *I Wanna Iguana*. New York: Putnam.

Pak, Soyung. 2001. *Dear Juno*. New York: Puffin.

Rylant, Cynthia. 2007. *Gooseberry Park.* San Diego: Harcourt.

Stewart, Sarah. 2007. *The Gardener.* New York: Square Fish.

BOOKS RECOMMENDED
BY THIS AUTHOR

Here is a brief list of books about writing workshop that you might want to look to after reading this text:

Bomer, Katherine. 2005. *Writing a Life: Teaching Memoir to Sharpen Insight, Shape Meaning—and Triumph Over Tests.* Portsmouth, NH: Heinemann.

Calkins, Lucy. 1994. *The Art of Teaching Writing.* Portsmouth, NH: Heinemann.

Calkins, Lucy, Amanda Hartman, and Zoe Ryder White. 2005. *One to One: The Art of Conferring with Young Writers.* Portsmouth, NH: Heinemann.

Calkins, Lucy, et al. 2003. *Units of Study for Primary Writing.* 7 vols. Portsmouth, NH: *first*hand.

Cowhey, Mary. 2006. *Black Ants and Buddhists: Thinking Critically and Teaching Differently in the Primary Grades.* Portland, ME: Stenhouse.

Graves, Donald. 1994. *A Fresh Look at Writing.* Portsmouth, NH: Heinemann.

Heard, Georgia. 2002. *The Revision Toolbox: Teaching Techniques That Work.* Portsmouth, NH: Heinemann.

Parsons, Stephanie. 2005. *First Grade Writers: Units of Study to Help Children Plan, Organize, and Structure Their Ideas*. Portsmouth, NH: Heinemann.

———. 2007. *Second Grade Writers: Units of Study to Help Children Focus on Audience and Purpose*. Portsmouth, NH: Heinemann.

Ray, Katie Wood. 1999. *Wondrous Words: Writers and Writing in the Elementary Classroom*. Urbana, IL: National Council of Teachers of English.